MEASURING VOLUME

By Julia Vogel • Illustrated by Luanne Marten

The Child's World®

Published by The Child's World®
1980 Lookout Drive • Mankato, MN 56003-1705
800-599-READ • www.childsworld.com

Acknowledgments
The Child's World®: Mary Berendes, Publishing Director
The Design Lab: Cover and interior design
Amnet: Cover and interior production
Red Line Editorial: Editorial direction

Photo credits
Sandra O'Claire/iStockphoto, cover, 1; Shutterstock Images, cover, 1, 2, 6, 15;
Tyler Olson/Shutterstock Images, 5; Don Nichols/iStockphoto, 9; M. Unal Ozmen/
Shutterstock Images, 13; Steve Snyder/iStockphoto, 16; Steven Collins/Shutterstock
Images, 19

ISBN 9781614732839
LCCN 2012933675

Printed in the United States of America
Mankato, MN
July 2012
PA02121

ABOUT THE AUTHOR
Award-winning author Julia Vogel has degrees in biology and forestry. Julia has four kids and a pint-sized pup named Nicky.

ABOUT THE ILLUSTRATOR
Luanne Marten has been drawing for a long time. She earned a bachelor's degree in art and design from the University of Kansas. She has four grown sons, and one of them often makes pizza with cups of flour while drinking a liter of pop.

TABLE OF CONTENTS

What Is Volume?

Have you ever asked, "How much?" How much medicine do you take when you are sick? How much milk goes in the brownies? How much water fills the backyard pool?

How can you find the answers? By measuring volume! Volume is the amount of space something takes up.

Knowing how to measure volume lets you do fun things—like help your parents make dessert!

People used handfuls to measure grains and other food for cooking.

ESTIMATE IT
How much is a handful? Take a plastic bowl to a sink. Turn on the water. Cup your hands and catch a handful. Count how many handfuls of water it takes to fill the bowl. Pour the water out and try again. Did you get the same count both times?

Estimating Volume

Long ago, people did not use exact measures of volume. They learned from practice how much water to put in the soup. They also learned how much wheat made a loaf of bread. They used clay pots, baskets, or handfuls to **estimate** amounts.

But pots and baskets were not all the same. People needed standard **units** to measure volume. This way everyone would get the same answers when they measured the same things.

Measuring Liquids

Since the 1800s, people in the United States have used the gallon unit to measure volumes of liquid. Apple cider, milk, and laundry detergent are often sold in gallon jugs. One gallon jug holds 1 gallon of liquid.

Let's say you have a bucket of water. You want to see how much water is in the bucket. You can use a **funnel** to pour it into a gallon jug. Does it all fit? The volume of the water is 1 gallon or less. Do you have water leftover when the jug is full? Your bucket has more than 1 gallon.

Some people buy milk in gallon jugs.

What if the water does not fill the jug? How can you measure how much water you have? You need to use smaller units. The **US customary system** has several units smaller than a gallon.

You may have seen a quart of juice in your refrigerator or a pint of ice cream in your freezer. A quart is one-fourth the size of a gallon. That means it would take 4 quarts to make 1 gallon. A pint is one-eighth the size of a gallon.

You can pour the water from the bucket into these containers. Then you can see if you have about a quart or a pint.

You can probably find quarts and pints in your refrigerator or freezer.

What if the water doesn't fill those containers? You'll need even smaller units. Cups might work. One cup is half as much as a pint or one-fourth as much as a quart. Sixteen cups make 1 gallon. Use a measuring cup to measure the water in your bucket. Count each cup of water you scoop out. You can place each cup in a separate bowl.

ADDING AND SUBTRACTING
Make sure you keep track of units when doing math. Two plus two does not equal four if you're adding 2 gallons and 2 pints. Remember, you have to add or subtract numbers with the same units.

Some measuring cups let you measure more or less than 1 cup.

Cooks and parents need even smaller units. They might measure a liquid in ounces. Eight ounces make 1 cup. Look at the label on a bottle of cooking oil. How many ounces are inside?

A tablespoon is even smaller than an ounce. There are 2 tablespoons in 1 ounce. There are 3 teaspoons in 1 tablespoon. You might know these units from taking medicine.

MEASURING SPOONS
A set of measuring spoons has spoons even smaller than teaspoons. There may be a one-half teaspoon and a one-fourth teaspoon. Those spoons hold a tiny bit. But cooks know that a tiny amount of some flavors is plenty.

14

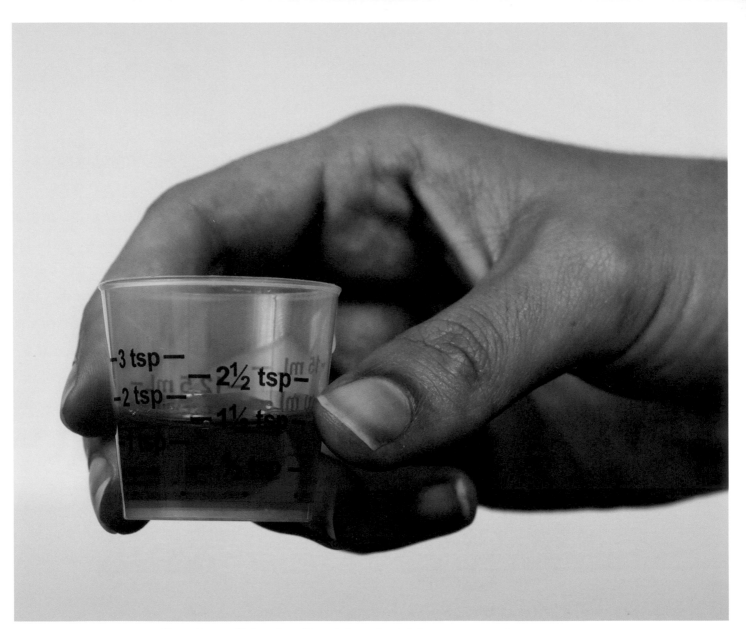

Cough medicine is often taken in tablespoons or teaspoons.

Soda often comes in 2-liter bottles.

LITERS AND MILLILITERS

Liter units are easy to work with. They are easily divided into smaller units. When doctors give medicine, they often use milliliters. There are about 5 milliliters in 1 teaspoon of medicine.

The Metric System

What a lot of units! The US customary system can be confusing. Most of the world uses another system. It is the **metric system**. In this system, the basic unit for volume is the liter. People in Europe buy liters of apple cider instead of gallons. One liter is just a bit more than 1 quart.

Measuring Solids

Solids can be measured by volume, too. A farmer's market is a good place to learn about the volume of dry solids. You can buy a pint of blueberries and a quart of peas. You can also buy a peck of apples and a bushel of potatoes. Even bigger amounts are a hogshead of sugar and a cord of wood.

See if you can spot pints and quarts the next time you are in a grocery store.

What Equals What?

Confused by all the different units? Here's a list to help keep them straight.

1 bushel = 4 pecks

1 peck = 2 gallons

1 gallon = 4 quarts

1 quart = 2 pints

1 pint = 2 cups

1 cup = 8 ounces

1 ounce = 2 tablespoons

1 tablespoon = 3 teaspoons

Practice learning US customary and metric units.

Measuring Mania

Now you can answer questions by measuring volume. You can answer how much medicine, milk, or water you need in teaspoons, liters, and more.

What other questions can you answer? Grab your measuring cups and start measuring!

You can help out in the kitchen now that you know about volume.

Glossary

estimate (ES-tuh-mate): To estimate means to make an educated guess to find out the value, amount, or distance of something. People used to estimate volume before there were standard measurements.

funnel (FUHN-uhl): A funnel is an open cone that narrows down into a tube. A funnel is used to pour liquids into a small opening.

metric system (MEH-trik SIS-tuhm): The metric system is a system of measuring based on the meter for length. Most people around the world use the metric system for measuring volume.

units (YOU-nits): Units are standard amounts used to measure. Liters, pints, and gallons are a few units used for measuring volume.

US customary system (YOO-es KUS-tuh-mer-ee SIS-tuhm): The US customary system is a system of measuring that uses feet, inches, and miles. The US customary system uses cups, quarts, and more for volume.

Books

Kensler, Chris. *Secret Treasures and Magical Measures Revealed: Adventures in Measuring.* New York: Simon & Schuster, 2003.

Maxwell, Yolanda. *Famous Bridges of the World: Measuring Length, Weight, and Volume.* New York: Rosen Publishing, 2005.

Schwartz, David M. *Millions to Measure.* New York: HarperCollins, 2003.

Web Sites

Visit our Web site for links about measuring volume: **childsworld.com/links**

Note to Parents, Teachers, and Librarians: We routinely verify our Web links to make sure they are safe and active sites. So encourage your readers to check them out!

Index

D1625548